CAREER EXPLORATION

Travel Agent

by Michael Burgan

Consultant:
Bill Connors, CTC
Director, Relationship Management
Institute of Certified Travel Agents (ICTA)

CAPSTONE BOOKS
an imprint of Capstone Press
Mankato, Minnesota

Capstone Books are published by Capstone Press
151 Good Counsel Drive, P.O. Box 669, Mankato, Minnesota 56002
http://www.capstone-press.com

Printed in the United States of America.

Library of Congress Cataloging-in-Publication Data
Burgan, Michael.
Travel agent/by Michael Burgan.
p. cm.—(Career exploration)
Includes bibliographical references and index.
Summary: Introduces the career of travel agent, providing information about educational requirements, duties, the workplace, salary, employment outlook, and possible future positions.
ISBN 0-7368-0492-7
1. Travel agents—Vocational guidance—Juvenile literature. [1. Travel agents—Vocational guidance. 2. Vocational guidance.] I. Title. II. Series.
G154.B85 2000
338.4'791'02373—dc21 99-049073

Editorial Credits
Connie R. Colwell, editor; Steve Christensen, cover designer; Kia Bielke, production designer and illustrator; Heidi Schoof, photo researcher

Photo Credits
FPG International LLC/T. Tracy, 20
Gregg Andersen, cover, 6, 9, 10, 13, 14, 16, 19, 22, 24, 26, 30, 33, 36, 38, 41
Unicorn Stock Photos/Jean Higgins, 43

2 3 4 5 6 05 04 03 02

Table of Contents

Fast Facts

Career Title	Travel Agent
O*NET Number	43021
DOT Cluster (Dictionary of Occupational Titles)	Professional, technical, and managerial occupations
DOT Number	252.152-010
GOE Number (Guide for Occupational Exploration)	08.02.06
NOC Number (National Occupational Classification-Canada)	6431
Salary Range (U.S. Bureau of Labor Statistics and Human Resources Development Canada, late 1990s figures)	U.S.: $15,000 to $34,500 Canada: $12,900 to $37,900 (Canadian dollars)
Minimum Educational Requirements	U.S.: high school diploma Canada: high school diploma
Certification/Licensing Requirements	U.S.: optional Canada: optional

Subject Knowledge	Clerical; Sales and Marketing; Customer and Personal Service; Sociology and Anthropology; Geography; Foreign Language; Transportation
Personal Abilities/Skills	Use arithmetic; treat customers with courtesy and respect; talk easily and persuasively to other people; help customers make up their minds about purchases by suggesting appropriate products
Job Outlook	U.S.: faster than average growth Canada: fair
Personal Interests	Understand and explain travel options; use arithmetic to total costs of purchases, compute percentages, and fill out forms; treat customers with courtesy and respect, even in difficult situations; talk easily and persuasively to other people, using language they understand; help customers make up their minds about purchases by suggesting appropriate products
Similar Types of Jobs	Secretaries; tour guides; airline reservation agents; rental car agents; travel counselors

Chapter 1

Travel Agent

Travel agents plan vacations and business trips. They help people find places to stay and things to do while traveling. Travel agents are called travel counselors in Canada and some places in the United States.

People who use travel agents' services are called clients. Travel agents ask clients questions about their travel needs. Travel agents then help clients plan trips. Travel agents help clients choose the best type of transportation to reach their destinations. Some clients may need to travel quickly by airplane. Other clients may want to travel by train or take cruise trips. Travel agents help clients choose where they will stay while traveling. Some clients may want to save money

People who use travel agents' services are called clients.

by staying at inexpensive motels. Other clients may want to stay at luxury hotels.

Travel agents also inform clients about travel activities. Some clients may want to see many sights while they are traveling. Others may only have time for one activity.

Travel agents contact companies that offer the services their clients need. Travel agents make reservations for clients with these companies. Reservations hold airline, cruise ship, or train tickets for clients. Reservations also hold clients' rooms in motels, hotels, or other places.

Skills on the Job

Travel agents should enjoy visiting new places. They should enjoy meeting people and seeing new things. Travel agents sometimes can travel for free or at reduced rates. They may take work-related trips called familiarization trips. These "fam" trips help agents learn about vacation spots or business trip locations. Travel agents use the information they learn on these trips to plan clients' trips.

Travel agents need good computer skills. Travel agents use computers to check the latest

Travel agents contact companies that offer the services their clients need.

prices of airplane tickets. They use computers to make hotel and other reservations. Travel agents also use computers to prepare itineraries for clients. An itinerary is a detailed plan of a vacation or business trip.

Travel agents need good communication skills. Travel agents must listen closely when clients discuss travel plans. Travel agents must record these details. This helps travel agents make the necessary arrangements. Travel agents also must speak clearly on the telephone. Travel

Travel agents must have good math skills to keep track of travel costs.

agents often must call companies to ask questions about their services. They then must give this information to their clients.

Travel agents must have good math skills. They must keep track of travel costs for some clients. Many clients are on a budget. They have only a certain amount of money available for vacations or business trips. Travel agents must make sure that clients can afford the trips travel agents plan.

Travel agents must have knowledge about the world. Knowledge about geography helps travel agents provide clients information about destination areas. Geography is the study of the people and places on Earth. Some travel agents speak more than one language. This helps travel agents communicate with people they meet while traveling.

Travel agents also must be able to get along with different types of people. A travel agent's goal is to help clients plan successful vacations and business trips. Clients who are happy with travel agents' work may use their services in the future. Clients who are unhappy may tell others about their bad experiences.

Where the Jobs Are

Most travel agents work for companies called travel agencies. Travel agencies often are located in office buildings. Travel agents who work at travel agencies are called inside travel agents. Some inside travel agents run their own travel agencies. But most work for travel agencies owned by others. Average-sized travel agencies employ about 10 inside travel agents. Some large travel agencies may employ as many as 100 inside travel agents.

Some travel agents work for travel agencies from their homes. These travel agents are called outside travel agents. Outside travel agents usually share their earnings with the travel agencies.

Some travel agents work for large corporations. Some of these companies require their employees to travel a great deal. These corporations often hire their own travel agents to plan business trips for their employees. These travel agents are called corporate travel agents. It is often more convenient for companies to employ corporate travel agents than to use the services of travel agencies.

Travel agencies often are located in office buildings.

MEXICO
HAWAII
Hawaii
Bermuda
Globetrotters
HAWAII

sky
Who's afraid of the Amazon?

Chapter 2

Day-to-Day Activities

Most travel agents work in travel agencies. Travel agents may specialize in certain types of vacations and business trips. They also may specialize in certain types of travel such as airplane or cruise ship travel.

In a Travel Agency

Travel agents who work for travel agencies must find clients. Many clients call or visit a local travel agency when they need travel information. Some clients hear of travel agencies through newspaper, radio, or TV advertisements. Other travel agencies gain clients through referrals. These clients learn

Most travel agents work in travel agencies.

Clients visit travel agencies for help in planning vacations.

about travel agencies through friends or family members.

Travel agents work closely with clients to plan trips. They may help clients decide on vacation destinations. A travel agent may have visited the clients' destinations in the past. Agents then can provide details about the location from their own experiences. Agents may give clients printed information about destinations. They may use computers to find additional information. Agents may contact local tourist offices in the destination areas. Most cities, states, and countries have these offices. Tourist offices may send travel information to clients and travel agents. This information can help clients plan their vacations or business trips.

Travel agents then make reservations for their clients. They call various companies and make reservations over the telephone. They also can use the Internet to make some reservations.

Travel agents may need to use a special computer system for trips that involve airplane travel. This system is called a computer reservation system (CRS). The CRS shows agents whether seats are available on particular flights. Agents also use the CRS to make reservations. The CRS uses codes for different cities and airports. Most experienced agents memorize these codes. Travel agents obtain airplane tickets for their clients after making flight reservations.

Travel agents also prepare itineraries for clients. These schedules show clients when their flights leave and arrive. Itineraries also tell clients whether they must change planes. An itinerary also may include information about hotels, rental cars, and other details.

Travel agents who plan vacations or business trips to other countries may have extra duties. These travel agents must know details about different countries. Some countries require foreign visitors to have passports. These papers prove that it is legal for visitors to enter foreign countries. Some parts of the world have diseases not common in North America. Travel agents must advise their clients about vaccines they should receive before traveling to these places. Vaccines are shots of medicine that protect people from certain diseases. Travel agents also must know about the different kinds of money and the different time zones used in foreign nations.

Inside travel agents have duties outside of the office. They may attend classes to learn

Travel agents prepare itineraries for clients.

about new destinations or computer systems. They also may speak about travel destinations to clubs and social groups.

Working from Home

Outside travel agents have many of the same duties as inside travel agents. They plan vacations and business trips for clients. But outside travel agents may not have access to

the CRS. Outside travel agents give reservation information to their travel agencies. The travel agencies then issue tickets for clients.

Outside travel agents may need to work harder to find clients than inside travel agents. Outside travel agents do not have offices where new clients can visit easily. Outside agents often rely on business from friends and family members to start their businesses. Later, they may use more common ways to let people know about their services. These include sending letters by mail or computer to local residents.

Corporate Agents

Corporate travel agents perform duties similar to those of inside travel agents. But corporate travel agents mainly plan business trips. Corporate travel agents do most of their work by telephone. They often take reservation requests by phone from corporate employees.

Corporate travel agents usually work in one of two settings. Some corporate travel agents work for large corporations. They plan business trips for other corporate employees. Other corporate travel agents work for large travel agencies.

Outside travel agents often work from their homes.

Some travel agents specialize in foreign travel.

These travel agencies often have offices across North America. The agencies often have their own offices inside corporations whose employees travel a great deal.

Specialized Agents

Some travel agents specialize in one type of travel. These agents are called specialized agents. Specialized agents perform many of the same basic tasks as other travel agents. But specialized agents are experts in one area of travel. For example, some specialized agents only plan cruises. They work closely with cruise lines. These companies own major cruise ships. The agents call the cruise lines to reserve cabins or make special arrangements for passengers. They receive information on new ships that are entering service. These travel agents try to match their clients' needs with the different cruises.

Other travel agents specialize in arranging tours. These travel agents may focus on travel to a particular part of the world. They also may arrange tours for church, school, or club groups. Agents who specialize in tours make all flight and hotel reservations for the group. They also hire tour guides and buses at the group's destination.

Travel agents and agencies also may specialize in other types of travel. Some travel agents specialize in vacations. Others specialize in business trips. Still other travel agents may specialize in foreign travel.

Sky
Who's afraid of the Amazon?
ETM
EMERALD TRAVEL MANAGEMENT

Chapter 3

The Right Candidate

Travel agents need a variety of abilities and interests. Agents should enjoy traveling and working with people. They also must be able to handle many daily tasks.

Abilities and Interests

Travel agents should enjoy traveling. Travel agents spend a great deal of time in their offices. But they also travel to learn about destinations. Travel agents should be curious about the world. They should want to explore other places. They should ask questions when they meet people during their trips. The agents then can share what they learn with their clients.

Travel agents should enjoy working with people. They must listen closely as clients explain their travel needs. Agents then must present choices for

Travel agents should enjoy working with people.

Travel agents must be hardworking.

clients. Travel agents must determine what type of trip will match their clients' interests.

Travel agents must be persuasive and hardworking. Travel agents must convince clients to use their services. They must work hard to meet clients' needs. Satisfied clients are more likely to use the travel agent's services in the future.

Work Style

Travel agents must deal with stress. Information about travel rates and schedules often changes. Travel agents must obtain the latest information from many travel companies. They need to remember this information so they can correctly advise their clients.

Travel agents sometimes must deal with unhappy clients. They may help clients who are trying to arrange a trip on a tight deadline. Travel agents sometimes must help clients who have canceled flights or other travel problems. Some clients become upset when they have problems with their itineraries. Travel agents must remain calm when dealing with angry or unhappy clients.

Basic Skills

Travel agents need good computer skills. Travel agents must be able to use different computer programs. Travel agents use word processing programs to type itineraries and letters. They access databases set up by airlines and other

Skills

Workplace Skills

Resources:

	Yes	No
Assign use of time	☑	☐
Assign use of money	☑	☐
Assign use of material and facility resources	☑	☐
Assign use of human resources	☐	☑

Interpersonal Skills:

	Yes	No
Take part as a member of a team	☑	☐
Teach others	☑	☐
Serve clients/customers	☑	☐
Show leadership	☑	☐
Work with others to arrive at a decision	☑	☐
Work with a variety of people	☑	☐

Information:

	Yes	No
Acquire and judge information	☑	☐
Understand and follow legal requirements	☑	☐
Organize and maintain information	☑	☐
Understand and communicate information	☑	☐
Use computers to process information	☑	☐

Systems:

	Yes	No
Identify, understand, and work with systems	☑	☐
Understand environmental, social, political, economic, or business systems	☑	☐
Oversee and correct system performance	☐	☑
Improve and create systems	☐	☑

Technology:

	Yes	No
Select technology	☑	☐
Apply technology to task	☑	☐
Maintain and troubleshoot technology	☐	☑

Foundation Skills

Basic Skills:

	Yes	No
Read	☑	☐
Write	☑	☐
Do arithmetic and math	☑	☐
Speak and listen	☑	☐

Thinking Skills:

	Yes	No
Learn	☑	☐
Reason	☑	☐
Think creatively	☑	☐
Make decisions	☑	☐
Solve problems	☑	☐

Personal Qualities:

	Yes	No
Take individual responsibility	☑	☐
Have self-esteem and self-management	☑	☐
Be sociable	☑	☐
Be fair, honest, and sincere	☑	☐

travel companies. Databases are computer files that organize and store information. Travel agents also may use the Internet to search for information about various travel destinations.

Travel agents must be able to obtain information from a variety of sources. They often use the CRS to gain information. They call people at travel companies by telephone. They also use books and other written sources of information. Travel agents must be able to use all this information to meet their clients' travel needs.

Travel agents must have good office skills. They must keep accurate records of their clients' travel plans. Travel agents also file the information they receive from travel companies. Agents may need this information to plan future trips.

Travel agents also must have good math skills. They must keep accurate records of the costs of clients' vacations or business trips. Travel agents also must keep track of the money they receive as payment from clients.

ETM
EMERALD TRAVEL MANAGEMENT

Chapter 4

Preparing for the Career

People who want to become travel agents need at least a high school diploma. Most agencies and companies prefer to hire travel agents who have some training in the travel field.

High School Education

High school students who want to become travel agents should take a variety of classes. Math, English, geography, and computer classes help students prepare for travel careers. Speech classes help students learn to speak clearly. Geography and history classes provide students with useful information about travel destinations. Business classes and foreign language courses also may be helpful.

Knowledge in geography provides travel agents with useful information about travel destinations.

High school students may work part-time at travel agencies. Students may work as receptionists or office assistants. These jobs can help students decide if they are interested in the travel field.

Post-Secondary Education

People interested in careers as travel agents may take courses after high school. Many trade or vocational schools in North America offer programs for travel agents. Students usually complete these programs in six to 18 weeks. Many community colleges in North America also have programs for travel agents. Students may graduate with either a certificate or a diploma. Some colleges and universities also offer courses in travel and tourism.

Students at vocational schools and community colleges take a variety of courses. Many of these courses are related directly to travel. Students learn about subjects such as fares and ticketing, travel industry operations, and geography. Students often have the opportunity to learn how to use the CRS. They also take classes in marketing and sales. These classes help them market their services to clients.

Students may work as receptionists in travel agencies.

Some large travel agencies offer their own courses for high school graduates. Smaller agencies also might employ high school graduates and teach them basic skills on the job. These students may become travel agents.

Trade Groups and Associations

Trade groups train many travel agents. These groups set standards for travel agents to follow. The largest of these groups is the American Society of Travel Agents (ASTA). Travel agents do not have

Career Requirements

High School Diploma → Post-Secondary Education

to join ASTA. But most travel agents become members of this group.

ASTA offers a course by mail for people who want to become travel agents. The group also offers continuing education courses. ASTA also can recommend travel agent programs at vocational schools and colleges that meet ASTA standards.

The Institute of Certified Travel Agents (ICTA) is another important group. ICTA offers a test called the Travel Agent Proficiency Test (TAP). Agents who pass this test receive a certificate stating that they have basic travel agent skills.

ICTA also offers two certificates. The Certified Travel Associate (CTA) is for travel agents with at least 18 months of experience. Travel agents must take 12 travel-related courses to earn this certificate. The second certificate is called the

Certified Travel Counselor (CTC). Classes for this certificate focus on business and professional skills. Agents must have five years of experience to receive the CTC certificate.

In Canada, the leading travel agent association is the Canadian Institute of Travel Counsellors (CITC). This group offers a program that allows travel agents to earn the title Certified Travel Manager. Counselors must have five years of experience to take this program. They must also meet standards set by the CITC.

Licensing

Most states and provinces do not require travel agents to have a license or be registered. The attorney general or Department of Commerce for each state has information on licensing requirements.

EUROPE
TRAFALGAR'S
Winter
BREAKS
TRAFALGAR'S
EUROPE
& BRITAIN '99
TRAFALGAR'S
USA
& CANADA
Europe
Canada
Ski
INSIGHT
EUROPE
& BRITAIN
U.S.A.
Ireland & Britain
Including Self-Drive Vacations
Europe
INSIGHT
EUROPE
& BRITAIN
Including The Eastern Mediterranean

Chapter 5

The Market

Travel agents work in agencies of many sizes. Some open their own agencies. Others work for someone else. Salaries and benefits depend on the agency's size and the travel agent's amount of experience.

Salary and Benefits

Travel agents do not charge fees to clients. They earn commissions from travel companies instead. These companies include airlines, hotels, and cruise lines. The travel companies pay travel agents a commission when a client uses the companies' services. For example, a client pays money to stay at a hotel. The hotel gives part of this money to the client's travel

Travel agents work in agencies of many sizes.

Travel agencies will continue to hire new travel agents.

agent. This money is the travel agent's commission.

Travel agents' salaries vary greatly. Salaries depend on the travel agent's experience and work location. Large agencies in major cities usually pay higher salaries. Agencies that focus on business travel also may pay higher salaries.

In the United States, most travel agents earn between $15,000 and $34,500. The average yearly salary for beginning full-time travel agents is about $16,400 per year. Agents with 10 or more years' experience can earn more than $30,000 per year.

In Canada, most travel counselors earn between $12,900 and $37,900 per year. The average yearly salary for full-time counselors is about $25,000.

Travel agents receive benefits in addition to salaries. These benefits may include health insurance, retirement plans, and paid vacations. Travel agents also receive discounts when they travel. Some experienced agents receive "fam" trips.

Job Outlook

Travel and tourism is the largest industry in the United States. Experts predict people will continue to spend more time and money on travel. Companies also will increase their spending on travel. The number of travel agent jobs is expected to increase faster than average in the United States. In Canada, the job market for travel agents is expected to remain fair.

New travel agents should find many job openings. Existing travel agencies will continue to hire new travel agents. Some of these travel agents will replace travel agents leaving the field. Others will fill new positions.

Travel agents may face more competition in the future. Many airlines and other travel companies sell their services on the Internet. Customers can get information and buy tickets without using travel agents. Some travel agencies may lose business because of this practice. Airlines also have lowered the commissions they pay to travel agents. This means that travel agencies must find other ways to make money. But many people still prefer to have travel agents help them with travel plans. Travel agents must keep up with travel industry trends in order to serve these clients.

Advancement Opportunities

Travel agents may advance in several ways. Some travel agents advance by moving to larger cities or travel agencies. Large travel agencies usually offer higher salaries and better benefits than small agencies. Large agencies also may

Large agencies may offer travel agents the chance to manage other employees.

offer travel agents the chance to manage other employees. Travel agent managers may make more money than other travel agents. The average salary for a travel agency manager in the United States is $23,000.

Other travel agents may advance by opening their own travel agencies. These travel agents keep all the commissions paid to them by travel companies. They also can hire other travel agents to work for them. But travel agents who own their own agencies must work hard to gain clients and sell their services.

Related Careers

People interested in the travel industry may find work in related careers. These people can become tour guides, meeting planners, airline reservation agents, or rental car agents. These careers deal with various aspects of the travel field.

People will continue to take vacations and plan business trips in the future. Many of these travelers will need the help of skilled travel agents to plan their trips. This will help career opportunities for travel agents increase in the future.

Travel agents will continue to help people plan their vacations in the future.

Great Escapes

Words to Know

budget (BUHJ-it)—a plan for how money will be spent

client (KLYE-uhnt)—a person who uses a travel agent's services

commission (kuh-MISH-uhn)—a percentage of a travel company's sales paid to a travel agent

database (DAY-tuh-bayss)—computer files that organize and store information

itinerary (eye-TIN-uh-rer-ee)—a detailed plan of a trip or vacation

passport (PASS-port)—an official booklet that proves that a person is a citizen of a certain country; passports allow people to travel to foreign countries.

reservation (rez-ur-VAY-shuhn)—an arrangement to save space or a seat for someone

To Learn More

Cosgrove, Holli, ed. *Career Discovery Encyclopedia.* Vol. 8. Chicago: Ferguson Publishing, 2000.

Eberts, Marjorie, Linda Brothers, and Ann Gisler. *Careers in Travel, Tourism, and Hospitality*. VGM Professional Careers. Lincolnwood, Ill.: VGM Career Horizons, 1997.

Miller, Robert F. *Travel.* Careers without College. Princeton, N.J.: Peterson's, 1993.

Milne, Robert Scott. *Opportunities in Travel Careers.* VGM Opportunities. Lincolnwood, Ill.: VGM Career Horizons, 1996.

Preparing for a Career in Travel & Hospitality. What Can I Do Now? Chicago: Ferguson Publishing, 1998.

Useful Addresses

Canadian Institute of Travel Counsellors of Ontario
55 Eglinton Avenue East
Suite 209
Toronto, ON M4P 1G8
Canada

National Tourism Foundation
P.O. Box 3071
Lexington, KY 40596-3071

Society of Travel Agents in Government
6935 Wisconsin Avenue NW
Suite 200
Bethesda, MD 20815

Travel Industry Association of America
1100 New York Avenue NW
Suite 450
Washington, DC 20005

Internet Sites

American Society of Travel Agents
http://www.astanet.com

Becoming a Travel Agent
http://www.exclusivetvlnet.com/marketing/schools/becoming.htm

Institute of Certified Travel Agents
http://www.icta.com

Job Futures—Travel Councellors
http://www.jobfutures.ca/jobfutures/noc/6431.html

Occupational Outlook Handbook—Travel Agents
http://stats.bls.gov/oco/ocos124.htm

Index